Unlock Your Potential

Secrets to Personal Growth

Table of Contents

1. Introduction 2

2. Discovering Your True Self 3

    2.1. The Importance of Self-Discovery 3

    2.2. Elements of Self-Discovery 3

    2.3. Techniques for Self-Discovery 4

    2.4. Embracing the Journey of Self-Discovery 5

3. Identifying Your Hidden Potential 6

    3.1. Recognizing the Existence of Hidden Potential 6

    3.2. Assessing Your Strengths and Talents 7

    3.3. Exploring Uncharted Territory 7

    3.4. Seeking External Feedback 7

    3.5. Investing Time in Self-Reflection 8

    3.6. Utilizing Personality and Aptitude Assessments 8

    3.7. Embracing Lifelong Learning 8

4. Overcoming Personal Barriers 10

    4.1. Mapping Your Barriers 10

    4.2. Overcoming Emotional Barriers 11

    4.3. Breaking Cognitive Barriers 11

    4.4. Conquering Behavioral Barriers 12

5. Embracing Positive Mindset 14

    5.1. Understanding the Power of Positivity 14

    5.2. Inculcating a Positive Perspective 15

    5.3. The Role of Affirmations and Visualizations 15

    5.4. Embracing Positivity in Everyday Life 16

    5.5. Overcoming Obstacles to a Positive Mindset 16

6. Mastering Self-Discipline 17

    6.1. Understanding Self-Discipline 17

    6.2. The Importance of Self-Discipline 18

6.3. Building Blocks of Self-Discipline 18

6.4. Practical Steps to Master Self-Discipline 19

6.5. Overcoming Obstacles to Self-Discipline 20

7. Practicing Effective Goal Setting 21

7.1. The Importance of Goal Setting 21

7.2. The BLISS Framework for Goal Setting 21

7.3. Cultivating the Habit of Goal Setting 22

7.4. Pitfalls of Goal Setting 22

7.5. Re-evaluation and Adjustment of Goals 23

8. Cultivating Healthy Habits 24

8.1. Understanding the Importance of Healthy Habits 24

8.2. Developing the Foundations of Healthy Habits 25

8.3. Crafting Your Personal Healthy Habit Plan 26

9. Building Resilience against Setbacks 28

9.1. The Essence of Resilience 28

9.2. Resilience as Muscle 28

9.3. Reconstructing Setbacks into Stepping Stones 29

9.4. Emotion Regulation and Resilience 30

9.5. Relishing Support Systems 30

10. Harnessing the Power of Self-Esteem 32

10.1. The Multifaceted Nature of Self-Esteem 32

10.2. Roots and Development of Self-Esteem 32

10.3. Role of Self-Esteem in Life 33

10.4. Techniques to Build Self-Esteem 33

10.5. Maintaining Your Self-Esteem in the Face of Setbacks 33

10.6. The Power of Self-Esteem: A Summation 34

11. Sustaining Motivation for Continuous Growth 35

11.1. The Nature of Motivation 35

11.2. Recognizing Your Motivation Source 35

11.3. Keeping The Flame Alive: Techniques to Sustain

Motivation 36

11.4. Roadblocks to Motivation and Ways To Overcome Them . . . 37

11.5. Cultivating A Growth Mindset for Long-term Motivation . . . 37

The only person you are destined to become is
the person you decide to be.

Chapter 1. Introduction

Welcome to "Unlock Your Potential: Secrets to Personal Growth," an energizing and transformational Special Report tailored just for individuals like you! Have you ever dreamt of tapping into that latent potential inside you, but weren't sure where to start? Then this Special Report is your perfect companion! Our not-so-secret treasure is rich with wisdom from leading personal growth experts, providing you with practical tools and actionable strategies to skyrocket your personal development. Brighten up your days as you journey through pages gleaming with inspiration and empowerment - they guide you to break free from your old patterns and step into a realm of endless possibilities. Remember, the door to your untapped potential is waiting, and this Special Report holds the key. Get ready to unlock the extraordinary you!

Chapter 2. Discovering Your True Self

The journey towards personal growth and unlocking your latent potential begins with a critical first step - discovering your true self. This process is not simply a surface-level introspection, but it is a deep, transformative exploration which requires courage, vulnerability, and an earnest desire to know 'Who Am I?'

2.1. The Importance of Self-Discovery

To seize your potential fully, it is imperative to understand who you are at your core. When we tread the path of self-discovery, we learn our authentic values and beliefs, recognize our strengths and weaknesses, comprehend our responses to various situations, and even unravel our deepest desires and fears. This holistic understanding forms the foundation of personal growth and transformation. It supports us in making conscious decisions aligned with our true nature, thereby bringing greater satisfaction and harmony in life.

2.2. Elements of Self-Discovery

The journey to discovering your true self is multi-faceted and encompasses various aspects. Here is an ascidoc list of the core elements:

- **Values:** Values are deeply held principles that guide our actions and decisions. To identify your authentic values, reflect on what truly matters to you, and think about the principles you won't compromise even under immense pressure.

- **Beliefs:** Beliefs are the assumptions we hold about ourselves, others, and the world. Identifying your belief systems can be challenging, as they often operate at a subconscious level. Regular introspection and mindfulness can help bring these beliefs to the surface.

- **Strengths and Weaknesses:** Recognizing your strengths and weaknesses is critical for personal growth. Play to your strengths and work on your weaknesses to become a more balanced and effective individual.

- **Desires and Fears:** Understanding your deepest desires and fears gives you insights into what motivates your actions or holds you back. It allows you to confront your fears and work towards fulfilling your desires with intention.

- **Responses and Reactions:** Knowing your typical responses to different situations helps you understand your behavioural patterns and emotional triggers. It aids in regulating your actions and emotions effectively.

2.3. Techniques for Self-Discovery

Several techniques can assist you on the path to self-discovery. Here's a detailed look at some of them:

- **Mindfulness and Meditation:** Practicing mindfulness brings your attention to the present moment, making you aware of your thoughts, emotions, and actions. Meditation can be a powerful tool for self-discovery, as it helps you calm your mind and look within with clarity.

- **Journaling:** Journaling helps record your thoughts, experiences, and insights. It encourages self-reflection and promotes deeper understanding.

- **Self-Reflection Questions:** Questions like 'What are my core values?', 'What are my strengths and weaknesses?', 'What do I fear most?', and 'What are my deepest desires?' can guide you towards introspection.

- **Personality and Psychometric Tests:** Various scientifically designed tests, such as the Myers-Briggs Type Indicator (MBTI), can provide you with insights into your personality traits, preferences, and behaviours.

- **Feedback from Others:** Constructive feedback from friends, family, and colleagues can often shed light on aspects of yourself you might be unaware of.

2.4. Embracing the Journey of Self-Discovery

Ultimately, self-discovery is not a destination, but an ongoing journey. It requires patience, humility, and commitment. This journey may bring about discomfort as you confront aspects of yourself you were previously unaware of or tend to ignore. Yet, with courage and acceptance, even these seemingly difficult revelations can become instruments of growth. Embrace this journey with an open heart and mind, and watch your life transform as you become the person you were always meant to be.

Remember, the process of uncovering your true self is like peeling an onion; every layer stripped back reveals yet another layer, offering a deeper understanding of who you really are. It's a continual process, but each step you take brings you closer to a life filled with authenticity, purpose, and happiness. This journey to self-discovery plays a pivotal role in unlocking your potential and setting you on the path to personal growth, paving the way for the next chapters in your journey – Identifying Your Hidden Potential and Overcoming Personal Barriers.

Remember - the journey of a thousand miles begins with a single step. And that single step, in this case, is Discovering Your True Self.

Chapter 3. Identifying Your Hidden Potential

The human mind and spirit hold an incalculable magnitude of potential, much of which remains undiscovered or unutilized. This uncharted trove of latent capabilities is your hidden potential; abilities that are reserved within you, invisible to the naked eye yet awaiting to be realized, to rain upon your life and radically transform it. It's akin to a dormant seed that carries the possibility of an entire forest, merely hidden beneath its humble exterior. In recognizing and unleashing your hidden potential, you'll be able to soar to unprecedented heights, paving your path to personal growth and achievement.

3.1. Recognizing the Existence of Hidden Potential

First and foremost, you must accept and recognize that everyone carries hidden potential - and that includes you. Too often, individuals shy away from this truth, trapping themselves in limiting beliefs. It's essential to escape the confines of these beliefs as they conceal your inner strength; your immense possible growth uncaptured. Embracing the idea that this untapped potential exists within you is the first stride towards unlocking it.

Understand that your capabilities aren't restricted to what has been manifested so far. There's a universe of possibilities brewing underneath the surface that's tied to your unique gifts and talents. Now, it's all about embarking on the journey of discovering and utilizing these dormant skills to their maximum potential.

3.2. Assessing Your Strengths and Talents

In order to identify your hidden potential, you must start by comprehensively understanding and assessing your current strengths and talents. Tapping into your natural capabilities can provide a clear indication of your inner reservoirs of potential.

You may want to take a pristine sheet of paper and list down skills or talents you are aware of, adding in any complements you've received or any areas others have identified as your strengths. Don't be modest here; remember, it's not about bragging, it's about introspecting and recognizing your innate capabilities. This process is essential as it forms a starting point from where you branch out and delve deeper into discovering what you're inherently capable of.

3.3. Exploring Uncharted Territory

Once you've outlined your known skills and talents, it's time to step out of your comfort zone and explore new territories. This might involve embarking upon unfamiliar experiences or learning new skills. Experimenting and putting yourself in novel scenarios instigates the manifestation of latent abilities. You'd be amazed by the multitude of talents you've unknowingly hidden, and the strengths you possess that had yet to surface.

Remember, the fear of failure should never be a hindrance in this exploration. Think of failures as stepping stones guiding you towards the discovery of your hidden potential. Always maintain an open mind, and let curiosity be your compass on this journey.

3.4. Seeking External Feedback

An outsider's perspective can often illuminate aspects about ourselves that remain unseen to our eyes. Therefore, seeking feedback from people who know you well can be remarkably valuable in your pursuit of revealing hidden potentials. This might include family, friends, or mentors who are familiar with your passions, strengths, and weaknesses. But be prepared, as some of the feedback might surprise you; it may draw attention towards strengths you've never credited yourself for, or hint at potential you'd never anticipated.

3.5. Investing Time in Self-Reflection

Equally important is the art of self-reflection. Carving out dedicated time for introspection can lead to valuable insights about your hidden capabilities. You could reflect on past experiences, choices, successes and failures, and pay close attention to patterns or recurring themes. This endeavor might unearth surprising revelations about where your potential lies.

3.6. Utilizing Personality and Aptitude Assessments

Making use of scientifically designed personality and aptitude assessments can further assist in your quest. Tools such as the Myers-Briggs Type Indicator or Holland's RIASEC Career Model can yield tailored insights about your personality traits and resultant potential. Such assessments aren't definitive, but they provide a structured way of exploring your innate strengths and inclinations.

3.7. Embracing Lifelong Learning

Finally, never cease to learn. Embrace lifelong learning and consistently seek to expand your knowledge and skills. In doing so, you constantly push the boundaries of your potential, continually discovering new layers to your capabilities.

In conclusion, identifying your hidden potential is a profound, ongoing journey of self-discovery. It invites a transformative process of exploration, assessment, reflection, and learning. By embracing this process, you unlock untold territory within yourself, truly maximizing your personal growth.

Chapter 4. Overcoming Personal Barriers

Understanding and overcoming personal barriers is nothing short of a Herculean task in the realm of personal growth. It might cause discomfort initially as you confront your darkest fears and insecurities, but the ultimate rewards are definitely worth it. Identifying your personal barriers and developing strategies to surmount those hurdles will help you finally break free from the cocoon of self-imposed limitations, revealing your brightly colored wings of potential.

4.1. Mapping Your Barriers

The first step towards overcoming personal barriers involves understanding what they are. Broadly speaking, personal barriers can be of various types, some of them being emotional, cognitive or behavioral. To arrive at a more precise understanding, you need to establish a personal inventory of your barriers - potential stumbling blocks that might be clouding your path to success. For instance, fear of failure might be preventing you from taking risks, or perhaps a lack of self-esteem is hindering your decision-making abilities. It might seem challenging at first, but an honest introspection will set you sailing in the right direction.

Developing this personal barrier map is essential as it provides you with a clear picture of what you're up against. It's like a roadmap, where your barriers are the obstacles, and the final destination is the land of succession and personal growth. The process includes identifying your limiting beliefs, ascertaining your fear zones, jotting down your unhelpful habits and coming to terms with unmanaged emotions. It's no easy feat, but remember - endurance is the very precursor to change.

4.2. Overcoming Emotional Barriers

Emotions are a double-edged sword in our journey towards personal development. They can both propel us forward or pull us back. On the one hand, they are the driving force behind our passion and love for something. On the other, they have the potential to overwhelm us, leading to inaction, insecurity, and despair. Overcoming emotional barriers requires a level of emotional intelligence that allows us to navigate our emotional landscape wisely.

One effective pathway to tear down emotional barriers is through developing emotional awareness. This is a skill that enables us to understand and name our emotions, instead of getting swept away in their torrential current. By keenly observing our emotional responses to different situations, we learn to build a healthy relationship with our emotions, accepting them, understanding them, and using them to our advantage.

Another critical part of dismantling these emotional walls involves learning to manage stress effectively. Incorporating practices such as mindfulness, meditation, exercise, and healthy nutrition can equip you with the ability to regulate your emotions, lessen harmful stress effects, and build emotional resilience.

Remember, it's not about negating your emotions but rather learning how to coexist with them in a healthy way. The better you can understand your emotional makeup, the more effectively you can work around your emotional barriers.

4.3. Breaking Cognitive Barriers

Cognitive barriers, including limiting beliefs and rigid mindsets, can act as silent saboteurs in our quest for personal growth. They are often manifested as self-defeating thoughts like "I am not good enough" or "I can't do this." These thoughts have the power to paralyze us with doubt and fear, thus, blocking our access to our best selves.

However, breaking cognitive barriers is possible with diligent effort and consistent practice. The most effective weapon against these barriers is the art of positive thinking. Cultivating a positive perspective can help you challenge these limiting beliefs and rectify dysfunctional thought patterns. You can start by practicing mindfulness, which involves being fully engaged with the present moment. It allows us to identify negative thought spirals and gently redirect our focus towards positivity.

In addition, setting small, achievable goals and celebrating your accomplishments along the way can gradually boost your confidence and help you overcome the cognitive barriers. Always remember that with every small triumph over a limiting belief, you move one step closer towards unlocking the full spectrum of your potential.

4.4. Conquering Behavioral Barriers

Behavioral barriers manifest as self-sabotaging behaviors or bad habits that stunt our personal growth. These patterns are often driven by deeply ingrained beliefs and thrive on your comfort zones, preventing you from stepping out and reaching your full potential.

To overcome these barriers, you need to instill new and more empowering habits. Firstly, you must identify negative patterns. Track your behaviors over a period – log what you do daily and review this for common negative patterns.

Once spotted, replace the unhealthy behavior with something positive. For example, if you have a habit of procrastinating important tasks, replace it with the habit of "eating the frog," which means doing the most difficult task first. This may sound difficult initially, but over time, you'll notice your ability to overcome procrastination growing stronger.

In conclusion, overcoming personal barriers requires a harmonious blend of emotional awareness, cogent thoughts, and positive behavior. It's a challenging journey indeed, but rest assured, it's one that manifests into more significant rewards. Always remember, every step that you take towards breaking your barriers, no matter how small, is one step towards meeting a better version of yourself, effectively transforming potential into reality. After all, even the longest journey begins with a single, small step.

Chapter 5. Embracing Positive Mindset

In the ever-evolving journey of personal growth, embracing a positive mindset is analogous to arming yourself with a navigational compass, experiencing the world through a wormhole that highlights paths of optimism, hope, and resilience. This chapter presents a comprehensive guide to helping you develop a constructive outlook that instills in your psyche the tools to empower your personal and professional life.

5.1. Understanding the Power of Positivity

Positivity is broadly acknowledged as an impactful force, an invisible hand that shapes our experiences, attitudes, and perspectives. A positive mindset is much more than just plastering a smile on your face or vehemently avoiding any thoughts remotely tinged by negativity. It's about illuminating your inner perspective that alters the way you perceive and respond to life's complex challenges.

A strong, positive mindset not only fuels your ambitions but also encourages an environment for wellbeing and happiness. Research by Barbara Fredrickson, among other psychologists, epitomizes this by introducing the "Broaden and Build" theory - positive emotions literally broaden your sense of possibilities and open your mind, which in turn allows you to build new skills and resources that can provide value in other areas of your life.

5.2. Inculcating a Positive Perspective

Creating a positive mindset is not a one-time endeavor but a step-by-step, consistent process of entraining your mind towards positivity. Challenging your thought patterns, questioning your belief systems, and refocusing your attention on positive aspects can seed a constructive mindset. Being aware of your thoughts, feelings, and actions can also reveal the interplay between your mindset and your reality.

One method is to practice intentional positivity, where you consciously choose to find the silver lining in any situation, regardless of how negative it may appear. This intentional emphasis on the brighter side of things rewires your brain over time to naturally gravitate towards more positive thoughts.

5.3. The Role of Affirmations and Visualizations

Affirmations and visualizations are powerful tools used to stimulate a positive way of thinking. Affirmations, positive statements about oneself or a situation, can transform your attitudes. They can zap away self-doubt, replacing them with self-assured, empowering beliefs. Meanwhile, visualizations prompt the brain to work towards fulfilling the visualized goal, enabling you to imagine the payoff of a positive mindset.

Remember, affirmations and visualizations aren't magical solutions. They are practical mental strategies backed by neuroscience that engage the phenomenon called neuroplasticity - the brain's ability to rewire itself by forming new neural connections throughout life.

5.4. Embracing Positivity in Everyday Life

Incorporating positivity in everyday routines can feel challenging, especially during trying times. However, engaging in regular physical activity, maintaining a healthy diet, seeking out social stewardship, focusing on gratitude, and giving without expecting anything in return are just some ways in which we can foster positivity.

Remember, even though we are aiming to build a positive mindset, it's perfectly okay to feel negative emotions. Positivity isn't about ignoring the reality but understanding that you have the ability to bounce back. It's about acknowledging the pain or discomfort, choosing to learn from it, and moving forward with conviction.

5.5. Overcoming Obstacles to a Positive Mindset

There will be times when pessimism eclipses positivity. During these moments, it's crucial to remember that developing a positive mindset isn't a linear process; setbacks and hurdles do happen. Being patient with yourself, accepting your emotions, and reminding yourself about previous victories or happy times can serve as a resilient bulwark against such barriers.

In the grand scheme of things, cultivating a positive mindset is about creating a mental safe haven – a space that harbors joy, gratitude, acceptance, and resilience. When we embrace this mindset, we illuminate the path that leads us towards the discoveries of our hidden potentials, thereby enabling the successful attainment of our goals.

Chapter 6. Mastering Self-Discipline

The art of mastering self-discipline lies at the heart of personal growth. Arguably, it is the cornerstone of a successful, productive life. This chapter will guide you through the process of cultivating this highly valuable trait.

6.1. Understanding Self-Discipline

Before diving into the means of developing self-discipline, it is necessary to have a comprehensive understanding of it. Self-discipline is the ability to control one's feelings, actions, and impulse to pursue what is right and essential, despite facing challenges and temptations. In other words, it is keeping your commitments to yourself. But let's dig deeper to uncover the traits that make up self-discipline:

- **Persistence:** Regardless of the hindrance, those who display self-discipline exhibit unyielding tenacity in the pursuit of their goals.

- **Delayed Gratification:** A crucial aspect of self-discipline is the ability to resist immediate rewards, holding off for a greater long-term gain.

- **Responsibility:** Taking accountability for one's actions is a sign of a disciplined individual. Rather than blaming external factors, acknowledging your part in outcomes exhibits self-discipline.

- **Consistency:** Progress is slow and gradual. Those with self-discipline understand this, maintaining a steady, consistent effort towards their chosen path.

6.2. The Importance of Self-Discipline

The significance of self-discipline has been emphasized by countless successful individuals and organizations. By keeping your actions aligned with your goals, you minimize wasted time, energy, and resources. Moreover, it's the driving force that helps you resist daily temptations—constant distractions that tug at your concentration and obstruct your progress.

Self-discipline is also key to maintaining focus during times when the going gets tough, when situations seem overwhelming and you start questioning your chosen path. Its influence extends beyond career achievements, shaping realms of physical health, emotional stability, and overall well-being. It's essential to steer your life in the direction you wish for it to go, ensuring you exert control rather than being at the mercy of external factors.

6.3. Building Blocks of Self-Discipline

Embarking on the journey to self-discipline requires a clear understanding of its fundamental elements.

- **Setting Clear Goals:** The initial step is identifying what you want to achieve. Crystalize your objectives, both short-term and long-term ones. Make your goals SMART—Specific, Measurable, Achievable, Relevant, and Time-bound. This encourages focus and gives you a destination to strive towards.

- **Creating a Plan of Action:** Once your goals are outlined, draft a detailed plan delineating how you plan to attain these objectives. This will serve as your roadmap, guiding your way forward.

- **Developing Self-Awareness:** You need to be in tune with your thoughts and emotions. Understanding your triggers and weaknesses lets you envisage and promptly address potential impediments.

- **Instilling a Growth Mindset:** Internalize the belief that you can improve and develop with effort and resilience. Adopting this perspective encourages perseverance despite failure and sees challenges as opportunities for learning.

6.4. Practical Steps to Master Self-Discipline

Having considered what self-discipline entails, we now delve into the actionable steps to refine it.

- **Organize Your Environment:** Your surroundings significantly impact your productivity and focus. Create a soothing, clutter-free space conducive to work and concentration.

- **Establish Routines:** Build a structured daily routine to reduce decision-making fatigue. This includes regulating your sleep cycle, meal times, work hours, and exercise regimen.

- **Use Positive Affirmations:** Bolster your discipline and focus by using positive affirmations. These short, powerful statements are designed to alter your subconscious mind and fortify a dedicated state of being.

- **Meditate:** Regular meditation builds mental resilience and aids in aligning your mind and actions with your ambitions.

- **Implement the '2-Minute Rule':** If a task takes less than two minutes to complete, do it immediately. This practice helps overcome procrastination and cultivates diligence.

- **Employ the '10-Minute Rule':** If you're having difficulty starting a task, commit to working on it for just ten minutes. Odds are, once you've begun, you'll choose to continue.

6.5. Overcoming Obstacles to Self-Discipline

Even the most disciplined individuals encounter obstacles. Being prepared for these hinders their ability to derail your progress, ensuring persistent advancement towards your goal. Mitigate these obstacles by:

- **Rewarding Progress:** Recognize and celebrate small achievements. This fuels motivation, making the process enjoyable and less strenuous.

- **Coping with Failures:** Slip-ups are inevitable, but they don't equate to failure. View them as learning opportunities, understand your missteps, and adapt your strategy.

- **Finding Accountability Partners:** Having someone to check in with enhances motivation. Whether it's a mentor, a peer, or a group, their support serves as an additional motivation to stay disciplined.

- **Adopting Stress Management Techniques:** Chronic stress can destroy your discipline. Incorporate stress relief activities into your routine, such as exercise, yoga, reading, or any hobby that relaxes and rejuvenates you.

Mastering self-discipline is a challenging, often grueling process, but the rewards it brings are immense and manifold. It propels personal growth, engenders respect in personal and professional spheres, and empowers you to overcome limitations, setting you on the path to achieving your dreams. This journey of mastering self-discipline will be an exploratory one, filled with self-discovery, determination, and unparalleled personal growth. Your journey starts now—armed with these insights, embark on your adventure towards a disciplined, fulfilling life.

Chapter 7. Practicing Effective Goal Setting

Goal setting is universally viewed as an effective tool to achievement. Goals offer a target for which to strive, encouraging you to organize your resources and efforts toward its attainment. Despite the unanimous agreement about the importance of goal setting, the process is often overlooked because many people simply don't know how to set goals effectively. This chapter demystifies the process of effective goal setting and helps you harness the power contained in its practice.

7.1. The Importance of Goal Setting

Goal setting is critical for several reasons. It allows you to take control of your life's direction, providing you with a benchmark for determining whether you are making meaningful progress in your personal growth journey. Moreover, goal setting harmoniously coordinates your focus and strengthens your motivation. It brings clarity, helping you to understand the end point of your aspirations and the steps necessary to arrive there, thus creating a guide for your whole decision-making process.

7.2. The BLISS Framework for Goal Setting

An effective method to set your goals is by using the BLISS framework.

1. Begin with the end in mind: Start by creating a vivid mental picture of your ultimate objective. This will act as your North Star, providing direction and helping you stay on track in your

journey.

2. Layout SMART goals: SMART stands for Specific, Measurable, Achievable, Relevant, and Time-bound. These criteria guide your goal setting and can significantly increase your chance of success.

3. Initiate an action plan: Realize your goal setting by laying out an action plan. This plan outlines the necessary steps required to achieve your goal.

4. Steadfastly commit: Commitment is the key to achieving goals. No matter how intelligently you plan, if you lack commitment and follow-through, your plan will end up in vain.

5. Stay resilient: The road to goal attainment is seldom smooth. You will face trials and tribulations. Having resilience to persist through these challenges is a pivotal aspect of effective goal setting.

7.3. Cultivating the Habit of Goal Setting

Cultivating the habit of setting goals can pay dividends not only in achieving specific outcomes, but also in enhancing your overall quality of life. You'll need to be patient and persistent, remembering that habits take time to form. Start with setting small, manageable goals and gradually stretch your capabilities. As you meet these smaller goals, your confidence will increase, giving you the impetus to aim for larger aspirations.

7.4. Pitfalls of Goal Setting

While goal setting can be astonishingly powerful, it's not without potential pitfalls. Setting unrealistic goals can lead to disappointment and frustration, potentially stalling your progress or reducing your motivation. Also, focusing too heavily on the outcome and neglecting the process can make the journey toward your goals less fulfilling. You need to celebrate the mini victories along the way to maintain a healthy and balanced mindset about your progress.

7.5. Re-evaluation and Adjustment of Goals

A crucial yet often ignored stage in goal setting is the re-evaluation and adjustment phase. It's important to review your goals regularly and make necessary adjustments based on current realities. While consistency is important, stubbornly sticking to a goal that is no longer relevant or beneficial could potentially hinder your personal growth.

In conclusion, effective goal setting takes more than simply declaring what you want to achieve. It requires intentional actions, resilience in the face of adversity, and a commitment to continually review and adjust your goals. Remember that goal setting is not a static activity, but rather a dynamic process that is to be woven into your daily life. Cultivate it, practice it, make it yours, and witness the extraordinary growth that follows.

Chapter 8. Cultivating Healthy Habits

Delving into the process of cultivating healthy habits, we open the door to a life-altering realm where remarkable changes can happen. Prosperity in life does not solely depend on talent or skills you possess; it equally rests on the daily habits that make up your existence. Sound habits are like tiny individual gears in the mechanism of a resilient clockwork, each critical to maintaining optimal functionality and moving the whole system towards set goals. In the grand scheme of personal growth, upholding certain behavioral patterns and daily activities turns into a potent panacea for stagnant development.

8.1. Understanding the Importance of Healthy Habits

For starters, it's significant to comprehend why cultivating healthy habits is crucial. As famously noted by renowned American Writer, Samuel Langhorne Clemens, better known by his pseudonym, Mark Twain, "Habit is habit, and not to be flung out of the window by any man, but coaxed downstairs a step at a time." These nuggets of wisdom reveal the momentous power of habits and emphasize the patience and persistence needed to chisel desirable ones into your life.

Fundamentally, our habits shape our lives, carving our days into templates of repeated actions and thoughts. They act as the auto-pilot of our daily lives, ruling about 40% of our behavior according to researchers at Duke University. Our habits manifest in every nook and corner of our existence - from the moment we rise from our slumber to the time we retire to bed, relentlessly influencing our weight, work, relationships, health, and happiness levels. Therefore, aligning our habits to healthier pursuits can drastically improve our wellbeing and furnish us towards personal growth.

8.2. Developing the Foundations of Healthy Habits

Once we fathom the significance of habits, it is crucial to master the science of habit formation in order to harness its power. According to the habit-formation model introduced by Dr. B.J. Fogg from Stanford University, habit formation is a convergence of three elements: motivation, ability, and trigger.

Your motivation refers to the desire to perform the habit. It is the driving force behind the action, spurred by a perceived intrinsic reward or satisfaction to be gained. Understand your motivations clearly and let them serve as your beacon when the journey gets tough.

Ability pertains to how easy it is for you to do the habit. The easier a task, the likelier you are to perform it. Therefore, it's suggested to start with small steps—known as 'tiny habits' in Fogg's model.

Finally, a trigger is an event or a context that induces the habit action. It might be setting your running shoes by the door, prompting you to exercise, or storing healthy snacks at eye level, leading you to choose them over unhealthy options.

Knowing the mechanics of habit formation equips you with the necessary tools to sculpt your habits in a way that enriches your life and parallels your personal growth journey.

8.3. Crafting Your Personal Healthy Habit Plan

Much like erecting a stable building requires a meticulous plan, establishing healthy habits demands a personalized layout that caters to your strengths, weaknesses, interests, and present circumstances.

Start by jotting down the habits you wish to embed into your daily routine. These could be: * Regular physical activity * Nutritious eating * Adequate hydration * Sufficient sleep * Consistent reading * Cutting down on screen time * Practicing mindfulness * Gratitude journaling

Once you have your list, use the SMART (Specific, Measurable, Achievable, Relevant, Time-bound) framework to refine your goals. For instance, instead of vaguely saying, "I want to exercise regularly", you could say, "I will jog for 30 minutes, three times a week, starting Monday."

Post identification of habits and goal-setting, focus on crafting an action plan using the Fogg Behavior Model. Gradually implement your habits and adjust as needed. Celebrate your tiny wins - as the saying goes, "Success is the sum of small efforts, repeated day in and day out."

Remind yourself: healthy habits cultivation is a marathon, not a sprint. There will be stumbles and setbacks, but they are just part of the journey. Instead of wallowing in failure and guilt, use these setback moments as a springboard for self-reflection and learning.

In conclusion, cultivating healthy habits is akin to harmonizing the notes in life's grand symphony. It's a lifelong commitment, a work of patience and persistence, but the end result can be breathtakingly beautiful and utterly transformative. By instilling wholesome habits, you are gifting yourself the opportunity to flourish both personally and professionally, to unlock the very best version of yourself. So, embark on the journey towards your healthier self, for it's an expedition worth undertaking.

Chapter 9. Building Resilience against Setbacks

In life, setbacks are simply par for the course. They can catch you off guard, shatter your confidence, and potentially erode the progress you've made on the road to self-development. Recalibrating after a setback requires a pivotal skill: resilience. Resilience is the capacity to recover quickly from difficulties; it denotes an inner strength and flexibility that enables you to weather life's storms and rebound stronger than before. In this enlightening segment, we'll teach you how to garner resilience and use it to navigate through setbacks, steering you back on course and propelling you forward to uncharted territories of personal growth.

9.1. The Essence of Resilience

No journey is devoid of obstacles. It's how you face and surmount these adversities that defines your resilience. When storms brew, do you sink or swim? Do you crumble, or do you stand firm, rising and soaring like a phoenix birthed from the fumes of plight? Resilience doesn't bloom overnight, it takes time.

To build resilience, one has to comprehend and accept that setbacks are inevitable. They aren't cataclysms sent to upend your life; they are essential elements of growth. When confronted with an obstacle or a challenging event, opt for a solution-focused view rather than concentrating on how hindering the problem is. Tap into the energy proclaimed by the setback and use it to your advantage.

9.2. Resilience as Muscle

Building resilience is similar to muscle building - you need to start small and progressively increase the extent of your exertion to reinforce strength. Start with minor hindrances and only escalate once you've mastered dealing with them. Much like how you wouldn't plunge into lifting heavy weights without an initial phase of lighter lifting, you shouldn't expect yourself to valiantly confront mighty setbacks without progressively tempering your resilience.

Take the time to identify the adverse events or issues that make you withdraw or respond negatively and ascertain what actions you can take to counteract these reactions. Endeavour to explore a kaleidoscope of coping strategies - this could involve mindfulness practice, focusing on healthy habits, positive self-talk, or seeking support from loved ones or professionals. Never underestimate the power of small steps because they aggregate into considerable strides.

9.3. Reconstructing Setbacks into Stepping Stones

Every setback presents a golden opportunity. Merrill Newman, a prominent resilience scholar, delineates resilience as "the process of adapting well in the face of adversity, trauma, tragedy, threats, or significant sources of stress". This definition exhorts us to rise from the debris of our setbacks, to transform them into stepping stones towards higher altitudes of self-growth.

Take each setback as a lesson to improve, a test to overcome, an experience to grow from. Treating trials as vehicles for learning cultivates a change in perspective – we no longer consider setbacks a ruination of our journey but rather an integral part of it.

9.4. Emotion Regulation and Resilience

An inability to manage your emotions can cripple your resilience. Emotional spirals can obscure the broader perspective, hindering your rationality and judgment and swaying your reactions towards negativity. Regulating your emotions, maintaining mental composure, and harboring a level-headed disposition, all sow the seeds for resilience.

By adopting mindfulness and indulging in practices such as meditation, deep breathing or yoga, you can maintain tranquility amidst tumultuous circumstances. Knowing when to draw emotional boundaries is equally important – don't allow yourself to be swallowed by the whirlpool of negative emotions. However, emotion regulation does not mean suppression; it's about understanding, managing and responding to these emotions in a healthy and productive way.

9.5. Relishing Support Systems

Resilience and perseverance don't need to be solitary battles. By having a robust support system, you aren't alone, and the weight of the world no longer rests solely on your shoulders. Be it family, friends, mentors, or therapists, encourage an open dialogue with these confidants about your struggles.

Don't shy away from seeking assistance or counsel when confronted by setbacks. Finding solace, strength, and encouragement in a community can unfurl vistas of hope, compassion, and optimism. You will find yourself heartened, and recognize that you are not defined by your setbacks, rather you are elevated by the resilience you demonstrate in the face of them.

Building resilience against setbacks is an enriching journey, one that shapes and magnifies your personal growth. By comprehending the essence of resilience, building it like a muscle, reconstructing setbacks into stepping stones, regulating your emotions, and harvesting support systems, resilience will not be a harbour that you reach after enduring the storm, but a firm mast that will guide you through it. Setbacks, then, can no longer stall your potential; they will fan its embers into a grand pyre, illuminating your path towards the extraordinary you. Remember, you are braver than you believe, stronger than you seem, and smarter than you think.

Chapter 10. Harnessing the Power of Self-Esteem

Before we delve into the intricate domain of self-esteem, it's imperative that we extract its definition from every angle. Self-esteem is the subjective evaluation of your own worth, or another way to put it - your self-concept. It's a belief and perception system that we create and carry about ourselves. Pioneering psychologists such as Carl Rogers and Nathaniel Branden have emphasized that self-esteem is a fundamental human need, vital for psychological health and well-being.

10.1. The Multifaceted Nature of Self-Esteem

As we begin to pull apart the mechanism of self-esteem, we uncover its numerous dimensions. Self-esteem can be explored in terms of trait self-esteem, which is relatively stable and enduring, and state self-esteem, that changes from moment to moment based on our experiences and interactions. There's also explicit self-esteem - the conscious and reflective self-assessment, contrasted by implicit self-esteem - an unconscious, involuntary form of self-evaluation. Each facet of self-esteem influences our behavior, choices, and even our relationships in different ways.

10.2. Roots and Development of Self-Esteem

Let's trace back to where and how self-esteem takes root. Childhood experiences undeniably play a fundamental role in shaping our self-esteem. Research suggests that a nurturing, supportive, and encouraging environment favors a healthy development of self-esteem. Conversely, factors such as criticism, abuse, punishment, or neglect can lead to impaired self-esteem, deeply affecting our mental health and perception of self.

10.3. Role of Self-Esteem in Life

Understanding the impact of self-esteem on our lives is critical. High self-esteem steers us towards constructive, confidence-boosting activities, strengthening our belief in our abilities. When we harness the power of self-esteem, we adopt a growth mindset, embrace challenges, bounce back from failures, and persist towards our goals with determination. On the other hand, low self-esteem might deter us from treading outside our comfort zones, impair our problem-solving abilities, foster self-doubt, and lead to risk-avoidant behaviors.

10.4. Techniques to Build Self-Esteem

Now, let's discuss the effective techniques to strengthen self-esteem. First and foremost, practice self-acceptance. Embrace your strengths, acknowledge your weaknesses, and be compassionate towards yourself. Second, identify and replace negative self-talk with positive affirmations. Visualization can also be a powerful tool in this arsenal. Furthermore, setting and achieving realistic goals, celebrating small victories, using self-help books or professional help if needed, and surrounding yourself with positivity are all potent tactics to enhance self-esteem.

10.5. Maintaining Your Self-Esteem in the Face of Setbacks

Despite our best efforts, life is unpredictable and setbacks are inevitable. When adversity strikes, the challenge is to maintain our self-esteem. It's essential in these trying times to remind ourselves that failures and setbacks are part of our growth process and aren't reflective of our overall capabilities. Practicing resilience, employing positive self-talk, staying connected with supportive people, and adopting a learning mindset help us bolster our self-esteem despite the setbacks.

10.6. The Power of Self-Esteem: A Summation

As we come to the close of this robust examination of self-esteem, it should be apparent that reckoning with our self-esteem is instrumental in leading a fulfilling life. Harnessing the power of self-esteem ignites the belief in our potential, empowers us to seize opportunities, fosters resilience against adversity, fuels intrinsic motivation, and shapes our life experiences positively. It's the backbone of our personal growth journey and a beacon in our pursuit of happiness and success.

Chapter 11. Sustaining Motivation for Continuous Growth

Motivation is an incredibly vital element in the grand endeavor of personal growth and development. It is the spark that can ignite your desire to grow and the force that can keep your metaphorical engine of development running. Without continuous motivation, the journey of personal growth could become an uphill struggle — it's like trying to drive your car without any fuel. Hence, sustaining motivation is a crucial component for continuous growth, and throughout this chapter, we will explore strategies, methods, and disciplines to do just that.

11.1. The Nature of Motivation

Motivation is not a one-size-fits-all concept. It's a dynamic and fluid force, and it comes in different forms for different people. It stems from our unique reasoning, our exclusive desires and personal ambitions, and it is catalyzed by our distinctive perception of success and fulfillment. It is essential to understand this individualistic nature of motivation — accepting that what motivates another person may not necessarily motivate you can help you navigate your own motivational landscape effectively.

11.2. Recognizing Your Motivation Source

The first step towards sustaining motivation is identifying the source of your motivation. Your motivational source can be your deepest desires, long-held aspirations, life objectives — essentially anything that drives you to take action. It might be intrinsic, coming from within you, driven by your personal interests or innate satisfaction, or extrinsic, where the motivation is derived from external factors, such as a reward. Understanding what motivates you is crucial because it guides you would to refuel and replenish your motivation when it runs low.

11.3. Keeping The Flame Alive: Techniques to Sustain Motivation

Despite the burning desire to achieve personal growth, motivation tends to waver over time. There are tangible strategies that you can employ to keep the fire alive. Let's delve into them:

1. Set achievable goals: Goals provide a tangible endpoint and give us a sense of direction. However, remember to set achievable and realistic goals, which encourage progressive achievements that can help maintain your motivation.

2. Celebrate small victories: Big goals are achieved by accomplishing a series of small ones. Every achievement, no matter how small, is a step towards your larger goal. Make it a habit to celebrate these small victories. It could be as simple as acknowledging to yourself that you did a good job; such recognition can do wonders for sustaining motivation.

3. Keep learning: Learning and personal growth are two sides of the same coin. With every new piece of information or skill you learn, you grow. Continual learning can keep the motivation wheels running since it fuels intellectual curiosity and personal mastery.

11.4. Roadblocks to Motivation and Ways To Overcome Them

Your journey to personal growth is not always going to be smooth sailing. There are many different roadblocks that can dampen your motivation.

1. Fear of failure: Fear is a potent demotivator. The fear of failure can paralyze, but recall that failure is not the end. Instead, view it as an opportunity to learn, grow, and hone yourself.

2. Lack of confidence: A lack of confidence can have a devastating effect on motivation. Enhancing your self-esteem is vital. Celebrate your small victories, acknowledge your abilities, and believe in yourself.

3. Procrastination: Often, the delay of action or the 'I will do it tomorrow' syndrome can dampen your motivation. The key is to start immediately, regardless of how insignificant your action might be.

11.5. Cultivating A Growth Mindset for Long-term Motivation

The final secret to sustaining motivation is cultivating a growth mindset. This concept of Growth Mindset introduced by psychologist Carol Dweck posits that abilities and intelligence can be developed through hard work, dedication, and the right strategies. It encourages you to view challenges as opportunities for learning, making mistakes as part of the growth process, and efforts as the pathway to mastery. A growth mindset can serve as a continuous source of motivation, keeping you persistent in your endeavors, resilient in the face of setbacks, and focused on the journey of personal growth.

Motivation is the lifeblood of personal growth and development. A consistent, replenishing stream of motivation enables you to climb the ladder of personal growth continuously. So, recognize what kindles the flame of motivation within you, protect it from the winds of demotivation, fan it with the techniques to sustain motivation, and above all, cultivate a growth mindset – your torch for the long, enlightening journey of personal growth. With this valuable knowledge, you are now equipped to sustain motivation for continuous growth, and surely, your journey toward reaching your latent potential will be both rewarding and fulfilling.